I0802564

Introduction by W. Terrence Gordon

In this remarkably rich essay, published first in _Explorations_ 7 (1957), McLuhan is a cultural and literary historian, but already ranging over themes that will later unify his media analysis. He draws on the massive research he conducted for his Cambridge doctoral thesis on Thomas Nashe, whose *The Returne from Parnassus* is quoted here. Also clearly in evidence from McLuhan's Cambridge years are his succinct and insightful comments on such topics as the relationship between written language and meaning, the interplay of ambiguity and auditory imagination. These follow an arresting opening paragraph cautioning the reader about the limits of metaphor. These themes form a bridge to McLuhan's reflections on the connection between Western languages and alphabetization and lead to the first articulation in his writings of the sensory effect of new technology and the semiotic reduction at work in all media: "And what writing couldn't make explicit, quickly got lost. Far more than writing, printing was a technological means of explicitness and explication." Readers of *Understanding Media* will note with interest here the linguistic analysis of dative-accusative forms in fifteenth and sixteenth century English in its relation to McLuhan's "ablative absolute" metaphor for the interaction of media. — WTG

The Effect of the Printed Book on Language in the 16th Century

No sense operates in isolation. Vision is partly structured by ocular and bodily movement; hearing by visual and kinesthetic experience. Visual space alone would be flat, but acoustic space is always spherical, a non-visualizable field of simultaneous relations. Yet it's a sphere only in its living dynamics, for it's neither contained in anything, nor contains anything. It has no horizons.

Factors making for simultaneous or instantaneous presentations of facts or forces tend to set up fields of relations which have an auditory character. Thus the telegraph supported auditory culture, even though its immediate result appeared as a visual one on the newspaper page. Similarly the photograph tends toward the auditory in giving simultaneously many facts which in writing or speech would take far longer to relate, and would have to be recounted, tear-dropper fashion, lineally.

Highly inflectional linguistic structures, spoken or written, have an auditory character; less inflected structures have a visual bias. Complexities of inflection, which for the ear constitute a means of articulation and order, take on a different character when translated phonetically for the eye.

Inflectional complexity, in written form, is not only burdensome for the ear; it's in conflict with the spatial order which the scanning eye finds natural. To the eye, inflections are not part of the simultaneous order of linguistic variations which they are for the ear. The reader's eye not only prefers one sound, one tone, in isolation, but it prefers one meaning at a time. Simultaneities like puns and ambiguities — the life of spoken discourse — become, in writing, affronts to taste, floutings of efficiency.

Shakespeare's 19th century editors tidied up his text by providing him with grammatical punctuation. They thought to bring out, or hold down, his meaning by introducing a kind of punctuation which came into use more and more after printing. This was an ordering of commas and periods to set off clauses for the eye. But Shakespeare's time punctuation was mainly rhetorical and auditory rather than grammatical. The 4th century grammarian Diomedes tells us that punctuation marks indicate an 'opportunity for taking breath', and Cassiodorus in his 6th century *Institutio de Arte Grammatica* notes that the *positura or distinctio* is a 'suitable pause in a duly measured delivery'. For them the function of punctuation for grammatical order was incidental to its function in aiding delivery.

This proportion of stress continued throughout medieval practice, though in passing on older views of punctuation, medieval writers allowed some recognition of punctuation for grammatical meaning. John of Salisbury in the 12th century noted in his *Metalogicus* that *positurœ* mark off the sense, but naturally included the grammatical in the rhetorical as the 'sense'. Whereas grammar and rhetoric were simultaneous for John of Salisbury, they rapidly became parallel, then remote from one another, as the age of print developed.

Classical-medieval theory and practice persisted through the 16th and 17th centuries. In his *English Grammar* of 1592 Ben Jonson simply observes, like any grammarian, 'A comma is a mean breathing, of the sentence going before, and following after . . . .' But print rapidly gave salience to the new visual role of punctuation for which no theoretic justification was forthcoming. To 19th century editors, classical-medieval components of Renaissance punctuation theory were invisible because they were, by then, overlaid by centuries of visual grammatical practice. Phonetic writing reduced the speed of word intake far below the level of oral delivery. Print raised the speed above the level of oral delivery. With phonetic writing came the tendency to read aloud and memorize texts, if only because to re-read them was so excessively tedious compared to the ease of oral repetition from memory. Slowness of manuscript reading necessitated capsulating authors via excerpts, sentences and summaries.

Oral disputation and multi-level comment on texts was a natural result of oral teaching. Multi-level awareness of linguistic phenomena and of audience structure held up during print's first century, but swiftly declined thereafter, since the speedy linear flow of printed language encouraged single perspective in word use and word study.

In More's *Utopia*, 1512, Hythlodaye justifies his refusal to set himself up as a counsellor to kings and princes:

> Your scholastic philosophy is not unpleasant among friends in familiar communication, but in the councils of kings, where great matters be debated and reasoned with great authority, these things have no place . . . [for] speculative philosophy thinks all things suitable for all occasions. There is another philosophy that is more urbane, which knows as you would say her own stage, and therefore orders and behaves herself in the play that she has in hand, playing her part accordingly with comeliness, uttering nothing out of due order and fashion.

Clearly, scholastic philosophy was a form of discourse which would not do in the new era. It was doomed, not because of its content or meaning, but because it was chatty, conversational discussion which took all manner of things into account at any given moment. In communication among friends it's natural to interrupt and to interject observations at any point. In such oral interchange there are numerous simultaneous vistas of any topic whatever. The subject is looked at swiftly from many angles: classic notions and insights concerning that subject are, via memory, on the tip of every tongue in the intimate group.

Such an oral form assumes encyclopedism, not specialism. With the coming of print, specialism developed because the individual reader by solitary effort could speed over the super-highways of assembly-line printing without the company or comment of a group of fellow learners and disputants. In his university studies on the 18th century Christopher Wordsworth records how written examinations were introduced at Cambridge when it became impossible for examiners to keep up with the individual reading and studies of their students. As books became cheaper, the quicker and more diligent students discovered that they could acquire knowledge for themselves where previous generations had been dependent on the oral teaching. Then arose the necessity of examination, and as this has come to be more public, and at last in a sense marketable, there has been a fresh demand for oral instruction.

The passage from *Utopia* indicates More's awareness that specialized matters of state, indeed the entire traffic of civil and public affairs, calls for single perspectives and 'due order and fashion'. A small amount of traffic permits casual mingling of animals, vehicles and pedestrians. Heavy traffic calls for strict regulation, whether of vehicles or language. The enormous increase in speed and volume of communication after printing taught the literate public the need for rules and decorum, in grammar, theater, the arts in general.

Medieval universities were not only oral in their procedures, they were little hampered by rigidities of administrative apparatus, nor were they grounded by the need for large libraries. Today young lawyers in setting up offices are advised to keep books out of sight: '*You* are the law, the source of all knowledge of the law, so far as your clients are concerned'. This was the natural attitude of student to teacher when books were few. It's becoming the attitude again when books are so numerous they are difficult to use or consult.

At Oxford under the Tudors, Mallet tells us, 'the old lawless democratic spirit yielded unwillingly to discipline. The Renaissance set up new ideas of learning'. The macadamized regularity of administrative procedure, which banished oral variety in prose by 1700, had begun to regulate school and college life much earlier. In place of the lively disputation, came the lecture – the single lecturer reading written notes to silent listeners who spent their remaining time in silent reading.

Print enabled one man to speak to many, whereas the readers of any one manuscript were few. Similarly print enabled one reader to read many authors in a few years with the resulting awareness which we now label 'historical'. One reader speeding through whole eras of the past could return with the illusion of having grasped the unified character of peoples or periods. The manuscript reader went too slowly, traveled too little to develop much time sense. Whatever of the past was discussed was felt as present, just as today the simultaneity and inclusiveness of our historical knowledge makes it all felt as being now. We have arrived once more at the oral via what appears as non-auditory means.

In 16th century dictionaries a word was cited in a series of usable phrases with authors indicated. No attempt was made to isolate meaning in a definition. Before print the very concept of word definition was meaningless, since no single author was read by many people at one period of time. Moreover, it would have been impossible for many people to have consulted any one lexicon. Medievalists say that even nowadays a medieval dictionary would be impossible since individual writers assumed they were free to define and develop any given term as their thought proceeded.

Print meant the possibility of uniform texts, grammars, and lexicons visually present to as many as asked for them. The classroom, as we know it, was entirely the by-product of print.

It was almost a century after print from moveable type began, before printers thought to use pagination for readers. Before then pagination was for book-binders only. With print, the book ceased to be something to be memorized and became a work of reference.

Individual writers throughout the 16th century varied tone sentence by sentence, even phrase by phrase, with all the oral freedom and flexibility of pre-print days. Not until the later 17th century did it become apparent that print called for a stylistic revolution. The speeding eye of the new reader favoured, not shifting tones, but steadily maintained tone, page by page, throughout the volume. It was a change of scenery comparable to that of the motorist who shifts from a road sprinkled with Burma Shave yelps and siren gestures from Miss Rheingold, to a throughway or turnpike. By the 18th century the reader could depend on a writer controlling the purr of his sentences and giving him a swift, smooth ride. Prose became urbane, macadamized. The plunging, rearing horses of 16th century journalese were more like a rodeo.

Ingenioso in *The Returne from Parnassus* says 'Ile have my pen run like a spigot and my invention answer it quicke as a drawer', while Nashe gallops breathless and inconsequential in a style calling for the utmost agility of mind and attention:

> Verie devout Asses they were, for all they were so dunstically set forth and such as thought they knew as much of God's minde as richer men: why inspiration was their ordinarie familiar, and buzd in their eares like a Bee in a box everie hower what newes from heaven, hell and the land of whipperginnie, displease them who durst, he should have his mittimus to damnation *ex tempore*, they would vaunt there was not a pease difference betwixt them and the Apostles, they were a poor as they, of as base trades as they, and no more inspired than they, and with God there is no respect of persons, onely herein may seem some little diversitie to lurk, that *Peter* wore a sword, and they count it flat hel fire for anie man to weare a dagger: nay, so grounded and gravlled were they in this opinion, that now when they should come to Battel, theres never a one of them would bring a blade (no, not an onion blade) about hym to dye for it.

A popular writer like Shakespeare was free of humanist obsessions about imitation of the ancients. He could exploit the old popular idiom and the huge new tapestry of polyglot effects that poured from the press. Many of his typical effects resulted from pouring the visual masques and pageants of the court and high-life through the new medium of spoken or orated poetry. The learned of the 16th century were not only obsessed by the need to imitate classical poets, but to adapt this verse to song. Verse had no status at all as recited. It had to be sung. Owing to print, spoken verse became popular on the stage. Song is speech slowed down and adapted to a single tone or pitch. Print made possible the rapid reading of verse. In speeding up song, print fostered oratorically delivered poetry.

While the learned devised laborious reconstructions of Greek theater in the form of grand opera, Shakespeare played with the new fabric and colours of the vernacular as enriched by a flood of translation from Latin, Spanish, French, Italian. When Donne and the Metaphysicals took over this new spoken verse for lyric poetry, they took over its heavy visual emphasis. So conscious were they of this visual stress, they reverted to the pictorial lore of the primitive *Biblia Pauperum.*

Between the 13th and 16th centuries word order substituted for word inflection as a principle of grammatical syntax. The same tendency occurred with word formation. After printing both tendencies accelerated greatly, and there was a shift from audible to visual means of syntax. Fries writes:

> In Old English this relationship of modification (the character-substance or modifier-noun relationship) was indicated primarily by means of inflectional forms. Thus in such a sentence as *on aenium otherum mystres thingum* it is quite clear the *otherum* must go with *thingum*, for the case form of both words is dative plural. We are compelled to say 'in any other things of the monastery' for plural. In Modern English *other* can be made to modify *things* only by being placed immediately before it.

It was not until the Middle English period that the collective noun singular in form appeared with any frequency *immediately* followed or preceded by a plural verb form. Collective nouns ever since, however, had in English a concord of number which depended on the meaning emphasized rather than on the form of the noun. In other words, the pattern concerning the use of number forms in secondary words that has emerged in the development of English is a concord based primarily on the number idea emphasized in the primary word rather than on its form.

Edward P. Morris, writing *On Principles and Methods in Latin Syntax*, says:

> The general movement by which single words have in part taken the place of inflection is the most sweeping and radical change in the history of the Indo-European languages. It is at once the indication and the result of a clearer feeling of concept-relation. *Inflection in the main rather suggests than expresses relations;* it is certainly not correct to say that in every case the expression of relation by a single word, e.g., a preposition, is clearer than the suggestion of the same relation by a case form, but it is correct to say that the relation can become associated with a single word only when it is felt with a considerable degree of clearness. The relation between concepts must itself become a concept. To this extent *the movement toward the expression of relation by single words is a movement toward precision.* The adverb-preposition is the expression in more distinct form of some element of meaning which was latent in the case-form. It serves therefore as a definition of the meaning of the case-form.

Now behind us are those unimaginative centuries which strove to eliminate ambiguity and suggestion from language in the interests of 'the one clear meaning'. Recovery of auditory imagination with its awareness of the total life of words has banished the tyranny of visual, printed forms of language with their intolerance of complex modes.

The inflectional suggests, rather than expresses or spells out, relations. Technology is explicitness. Writing was a huge technological advance in this respect. It expressed, it made explicit, many relations which were implicit, suggested in inflectional language structures. And what writing couldn't make explicit, quickly got lost. Far more than writing, printing was a technological means of explicitness and explication. But those auditory inflections and relations which could not be made visually explicit by print were soon lost to the language — except for dialects and Vulgar English, of course.

As a result of these changes there remain in English only six forms (me, us, him, them, her, whom) to distinguish the dative or the accusative from the nominative, and the six case forms of these pronouns in their modern use do not function in the conveying of grammatical ideas. These are the words that create most of the booby-traps of English for the semi-literate. The whole problem is to manage their auditory patterns in relation to a half-learned visual or word-position grammar. As with punctuation straddling between a rhetorical and a syntactical function, so with these relics of auditory and inflectional English. Their users are unaware that the trick is to ignore the visual relations of words when handling these mavericks. This confusion is true of the other forms as well. Fries writes:

> The growing importance of word order as a grammatical device to show the relation between substantive and verb since the early 15th century has had an important effect upon the use of these six dative-accusative forms. Certain positions in the English sentence have come to be felt as 'subject' territory, others as 'object' territory and the forms of the words in each territory are pressed to adjust themselves to the character of that territory. The dative-accusative forms, with no real function of their own but used only as an accompaniment of other devices offer very little resistance to the pressures of word order. Our Modern English 'I was given a book' furnished a good illustration of the pressure of word order. The Old English 'Me waes gegeifen an boc', with the da-

tive pronoun standing first, was a common construction. It is only after word order had become a vigorous device for the showing of grammatical relationships that the dative *me* standing in 'subject' territory was changed to the nominative *I*. Ever since the 16th century this new construction has been normal English practice in spite of the protests of certain grammarians. The dative with impersonal verbs which appeared frequently in Old and Middle English also shows the pressure of word order as these constructions were replaced by the nominative form of the pronoun and the personal verb. *Him likod* became *He liked. Me greues* became *I grieve.* Altogether it is only in the few places where the pressures of word order conflict with the inertia of an older practice that problems arise concerning the use of these case forms of pronouns. In nearly all situations the older practice concerning the inflections (similar to that of Latin) agrees with the newer pressures of word order.

In the matter of person, the distinct verb forms have tended to disappear and no new device has taken their place; in the matter of mood, however, the passing of the inflections has been accompanied by a greatly increased use of the so-called modal auxiliaries—the function words used to express an emotional attitude toward the action or state. In Old English there were distinctive verb forms for the subjunctive in both the present tense and the preterit. Within the subjunctive singular and plural number forms were clearly separated, but there were no forms to distinguish person. These distinctive subjunctive forms, in the course of our language development, fell together with those of the indicative mode, until, in Present-day English, but one form remains, in all verbs except the verb *to be*, to separate subjunctive mood from indicative. In Present-day English, as in the past, the subjunctive has no distinct forms for the various persons, whereas the indicative still retains the -s of the third person singular. As a matter of fact, however, this s-less subjunctive very rarely appears, and then in Vulgar English: 'So *help* me God', 'God *bless* you and *speed* you on', 'insisted that he join the army'.

Only the indicative remains and what could be more striking about its one-level lineality than the fact we have altered the meaning of the word from *dico* to pointing or indicating in a non-auditory mode. Once the dynamics of language begin to shift to the visual mode, past, present, and future become the only time senses that make sense, because they are the only ones that can be indicated to the reader of a page. All those subtle time and mood relations natural to pre-literate language and to the simultaneous order of the auditory language are swiftly sheared away by the assembly lines of the typesetter.

The explicit technology of written and especially printed codifications of language inherently favours any tendency to develop or utilize monosyllables as a source of new word formation. Everything we know about technology points to its natural bent for the replaceable part and the snug unit that can serve many roles.

The disappearance of the final *-e*, still retained by most verb forms till the 15th century, released many words to function both as noun and verb. This development gave great flexibility to 16th century usage, but was not peculiar to that period, having continued unabated. In fact, the newspaper headline jungle is probably richer today in words with dual noun-verb functions than the Elizabethan period. Monosyllabism has been given more development by newspaper headlines than by all other factors combined. With headlines, the purely visual aspect of print accelerated rather than originated. But the headline only gives acute stress to factors inherent in phonetic writing, emergent in print, and obvious in the newspaper:

EPSOM SALTS WON'T WORK
STIX NIX HIX PIX
BERRA'S BIG BAT BANISHES BUMS
LONDON FIDDLES WHILE BURNS ROAMS
UNDERCOVER MEN UNCOVER UNDERWEAR UNDERWORLD

While the power press, fed by the telegraph, frantically promoted monosyllabism and action verb headlines, literary men were justifying this development by theories about the superiority of simple colloquial Anglo-Saxon English. Jespersen writes of the phenomenon of back-formation which occurs entirely as a result of word appearance: 'The adverbs *sideling*, *groveling* and *darkling* were originally formed by means of the adverbial ending *-ling*, but in such phrases as "he walks sideling", "he lies groveling", etc., they looked exactly like participles in *-ing*, and the consequence was that the new verbs to sidle, to grovel, and to darkle were derived from them by the subtraction of *-ing*.' But why should it be only in some trivial backwater of back-formation that the Jespersens notice the power of visuality in linguistic change?

Printed grammars since the 18th century created a fog based on the concept of correctness. Once this concept, unconsciously derived from the form of print itself, was pervasive, any hope of study of the actual dynamics of our language situation was obliterated. Our new media with their complex influence on language are similarly blanketed today.

The Effect of the Printed Book on Language in the 16th Century
Marshall McLuhan - Unbound (02)

ISBN: 1-58423-051-7
Library of Congress Control Number 2005927213

Marshall McLuhan Unbound Project Editors
Eric McLuhan, W. Terrence Gordon

Published in United States in October 2005 by
Gingko Press, Inc.
5768 Paradise Drive, Suite J • Corte Madera, CA 94925
(415) 924-9615 • Fax (415) 924-9608
email: books@gingkopress.com
http://www.gingkopress.com

© The Estate of Mashall McLuhan. www.marshallmcluhan.com

Introduction to "The Effect of the Printed Book on Language in the 16th Century"
© W. Terrence Gordon

Design, packaging and production: Die Gestalten Verlag, Berlin
Layout and Typography: onlab, Berlin
Fonts: *Dolly* by Underware, *Bullet* by House Industries
Production: Martin Bretschneider, Vinzenz Geppert
Art direction: Robert Klanten

Made in Germany

All rights reserved. No part of this essay may be used or reproduced in any manner whatsoever without written permission from the publisher except in the case of brief quotations embodied in critical articles and reviews. For information address Gingko Press.